# The Consultation

**Dedicated to God**

# The Consultation

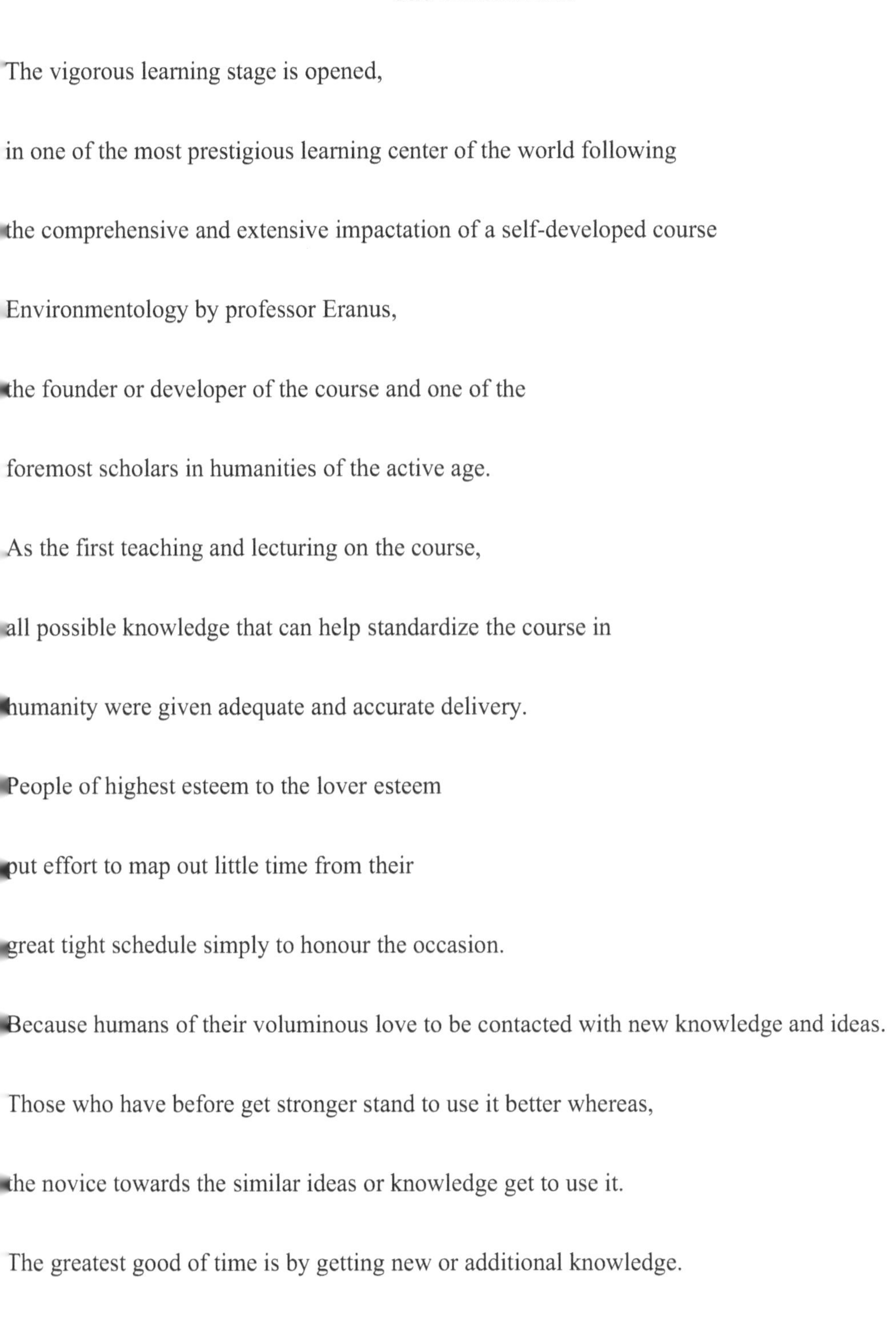

The vigorous learning stage is opened,

in one of the most prestigious learning center of the world following

the comprehensive and extensive impactation of a self-developed course

Environmentology by professor Eranus,

the founder or developer of the course and one of the

foremost scholars in humanities of the active age.

As the first teaching and lecturing on the course,

all possible knowledge that can help standardize the course in

humanity were given adequate and accurate delivery.

People of highest esteem to the lover esteem

put effort to map out little time from their

great tight schedule simply to honour the occasion.

Because humans of their voluminous love to be contacted with new knowledge and ideas.

Those who have before get stronger stand to use it better whereas,

the novice towards the similar ideas or knowledge get to use it.

The greatest good of time is by getting new or additional knowledge.

This helps to clearly distinguishes humans among others.

New knowledge renders divergent stands for exploit

and it is the hallmark of advancement, singularly and plurality.

The ground for knowledge transaction is ever decorated

with light atmosphere upon beautiful appearances.

The joy of any teacher is to have serious learners so as it is on the opposite.

This is surely the first major consideration on the

platform of knowledge impactation and acquisition.

The both can't do without one another.

Levels in life are measure by experience and understanding.

Experience is measured by the possible prevailing and useful

information gathered and understanding is the appropriations

given to information gathered for the benefit of humanity.

Anyone encircled with the above is eligible and a right candidate to be honoured,

recommended and emulated in life.

Such person can be a consultant in the area of his or her mastery.

Professor Eranus is found on this.

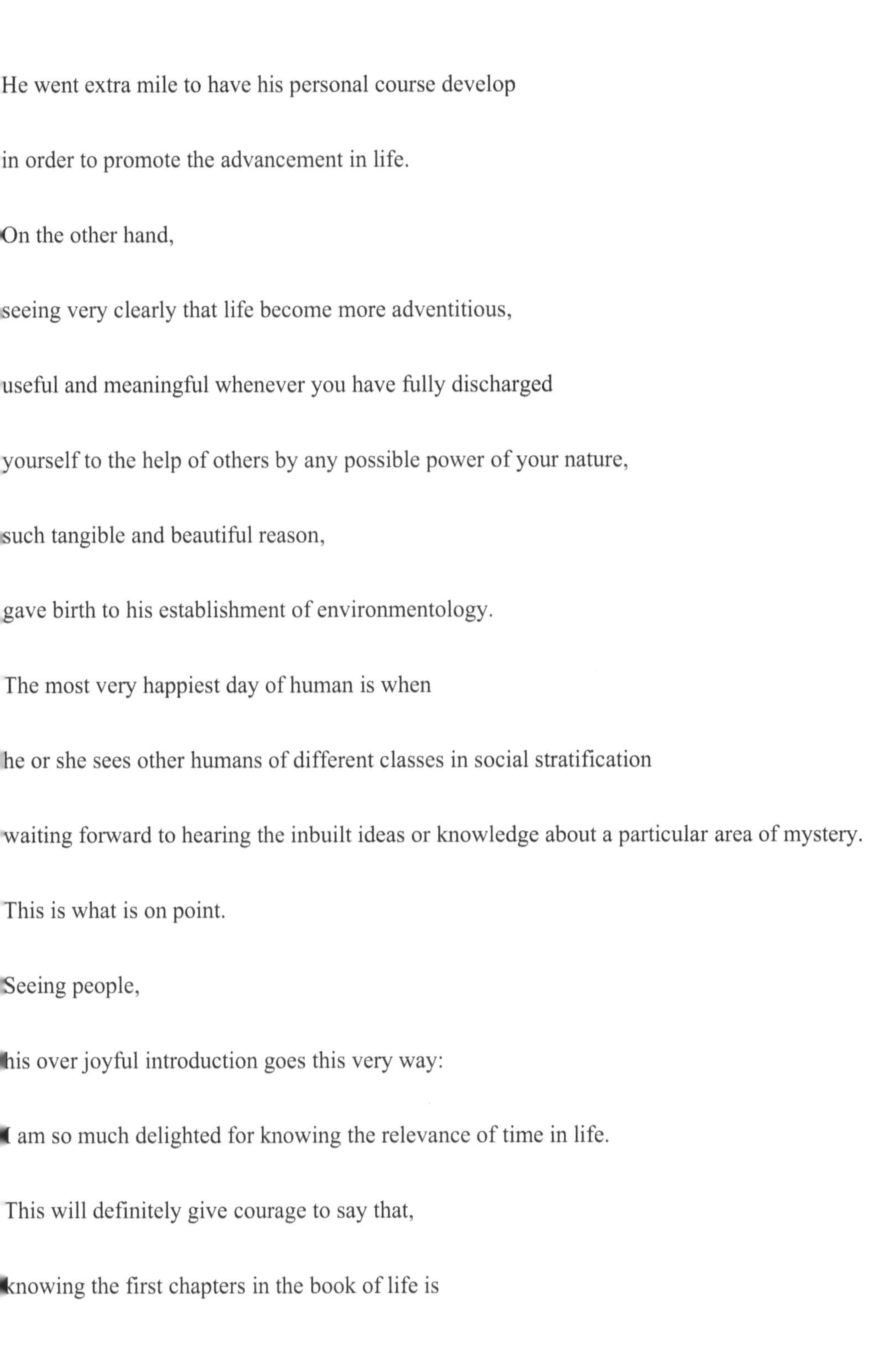

He went extra mile to have his personal course develop

in order to promote the advancement in life.

On the other hand,

seeing very clearly that life become more adventitious,

useful and meaningful whenever you have fully discharged

yourself to the help of others by any possible power of your nature,

such tangible and beautiful reason,

gave birth to his establishment of environmentology.

The most very happiest day of human is when

he or she sees other humans of different classes in social stratification

waiting forward to hearing the inbuilt ideas or knowledge about a particular area of mystery.

This is what is on point.

Seeing people,

his over joyful introduction goes this very way:

I am so much delighted for knowing the relevance of time in life.

This will definitely give courage to say that,

knowing the first chapters in the book of life is

identifying right time for purposes and the last chapters in the book of life is death,

having knowing this must be the core reason behind your beautiful appearances,

therefore,

I must salute your good effort.

The joy of all humans is to dominate all possible areas of life.

Good knowledge is the genesis of right dominancy.

Remember that everything has two sides:

the harmful and the harmless parts.

It is very tantamount to adhere to fact that effects

are the real distinguishers of good and bad and this only happen under the influence of time.

So, getting knowledge is not necessarily enough.

But the most concern should be on how to affect the

humanity with such knowledge through right methods and applications.

In life,

experience and research have better knowledge about people

who only love to be identified in a particular place,

some are very good to be known on how they affects

ives in a particular place whereas some are never courageous

to be known in any particular place.

The power to manifest,

identify and know is the major concerns in life.

Anyone that embraces the three is suitable to be celebrated,

anyone who embraces the two out of the three is to be recognized

while anyone who don't embraces anyone among is not to be

considered as a right sensible person.

I am not better or more than you in any way but the

respect you give about advancing the humanity is the reason behind your appearances.

And I must do respect you for that by all means.

Time is the paramount host of life.

So, whosoever plays with time,

directly and indirectly plays with life.

Only the knowledgeable people do know the value of life.

Therefore, I might take another look if I do learn to play with time or life, as usually.

The major purpose of life is to make changes

and the major goals for changes is advancement and betterment.

Many reasons might arise in your mind towards my very handiwork,

but I truly tell you to uphold to this fact behind my very handiwork.

Thank you ones again because,

without you,

I can truly do nothing.

I don't think anyone will be proud enough to tell me among you that,

your present state of being is gotten by your personal efforts.

I am sure no one can't boast of that.

To me, I consider humans as the most rewarding being

and phenomenon for both heaven and earth.

And on this very sense,

I can say, both the heaven and the earth would have not come to

stay after a month of their creations by the creator of all creatures.

Therefore, the activities of human are the only reason behind the

continuous existence of heaven and earth.

God himself can't stay without human as

He will no longer have any work to do if there is no human.

And for this reason,

God use the whole day and the last day to create His like.

Apart from His words which are His representatives,

He likes nothing more than humans in all His creatures.

This is the sole reason why I say I can't do without you.

To effectively and effectually manage the time,

let me go straight to the business of the day.

And before we go into that,

I will love to indicted my readiness to serve as a

consultant on this course throughout my life time and the reason being that,

as a course that directly deals with human interactions

between one another and other creatures to keep better

understanding for harmonious environment,

we have different people on a basis of different situations and therefore,

there must be a possible controversies in discharging the course ideals

to better your state of being with others in a society.

Now to the main business: environmentology is the study of activities that make up possible state of human being in an environment in reference to appropriate actions applied to get expected result on such desire.

The subject is very familiar as it is strongly denotative in nature.

Life is a total activities appreciated.

As humans are different from one another,

so as they have different desired activities.

Therefore, there must be little or big controversies in the domain.

Activities of humans are not far from what they can see and imagine around them.

That is why we simply have different lives to as different humans.

There are numerous violations in human activities due to worldly chains

that fight human desires.

The hope on activities leads to the genesis of disappointment.

Because, transactions between two or more persons

can never have expected result as the sole reason

for human actions are ever personal and selfish.

Humans have time to distinguish foolish from wise and for this,

all humans desire to be wiser than their opponents.

In this fight, there can never be standard cooperation.

So, arriving at a compromise must duly accomplish equal percentage.

If people are given equal percentage,

there is no wider room to succeed one another.

In regards to all these points,

the course will definitely get it relevance.

The components of the course are: trust, betray, happiness and sorrow.

As you meet humans,

some are very good in keeping agreements,

some are very good in betraying agreements,

some are very good in keeping normal lifestyles with others no matter what happen,

and some are very good in extending happy life with others

while some are very good in keeping and extending sorrow with life with others.

The laws of the course are:

try to be simple with simple situations,

be hard with hard situations,

make sure time is appropriated with right situations,

make sure time is inappropriate with wrong situations,

time for seriousness differ from time for play,

deal with people accordingly to have desire result,

don't take good for bad otherwise treated and noted,

don't take bad for good otherwise treated and noted,

try to be good in your desired arena and be conscious with any progress in life.

The principles of the course are: try to embrace the latest styles of doing things,

try to go extra mile to achieve your desire,

only when you are adequately equipped you can go for such exercise,

try new and strange things yourself, and try to ever be in-charge.

Methods of the course are:

direct, indirect and alternative.

You must know that the activities of life have plenty channels.

So, to enjoy the dividend of life,

you must be skillfully active to master all areas and methods

the pleasure of activities are gained.

Life wait for no one, so as,

don't wait for life to choose way for you.

It might be late if you can wait.

Get it right also that,

life can't give you right directions following divergent forces behind it existence.

You must therefore fight for appropriate method towards any given activities.

This is the strong determinant of achievement in human activities.

The scope of the course is to identify relevant ways to meet up

with desires on any given activities of life,

to know the difference that uphold life's activities,

for human to appropriate ways for

possible reasons behind changes of environmental activities,

for human to gain dormancy in all desired activities and

to manifest mastery in achieving things.

The elements of the course are:

ideas, knowledge, similarities, comparisms, differentiations, understanding and wisdom.

It is very paramount to know humans on the grounds of the above.

You can never successfully do anything reasonable,

useful and meaningful against or for any person without identifying

the above in the particular person,

because, there are the possible and the

very prevailing directions to make transactions in order

to meet up your desire concerning any given activities on such matter.

So, the foremost embracer should be knowledgeable about the particular thing or person.

You can then use others to standardize your trade on the thing or person.

The slogan of the course is

"create or destroy under the power of time and under different umbrella of human".

The types of the course are:

day environmentology which deals with the possible human activities that take place during the daytime,

night environmentology which deals with the possible human activities that take place during the night,

appropriate environmentology which deals with the possible human activities that take place for the benefit of humanity

and inappropriate environmentology which deals with the possible activities of human that take place for the harm of humanity.

Time in life is segmented as human activities are also categorized.

Life does not have similar equality in two things or more.

Activities can happen anytime and anywhere, because,

only the effect is the major concern of humanity.

However, there are some activities that are best known to happen during the day,

some do best happen during the night,

some are favourable in nature and some are harmful in nature.

We have this because powers behind activities in relation

to a particular period of time are strongly consider in regards to effects.

The theories of the course are:

theory of motivation, theory of compatibility, theory of knowledge and theory of application and theory of time and theory of human.

These are identified for the purposes and effects of activities in humanity.

It is expected that questions prompt more understanding and a gateway to further studies.

Lecturing and teaching is not completed with questions and knowledge is not appropriated or gain without answers.

This shows the mastery of acquisitions and impartations.

So, after the words of professor Eranus,

the following questions were asked and answered squarely.

The first question goes:

what are the necessary safeties in going closer

to your open and secret enemies and what are the necessary

dangers in going closer to your open and secret enemies,

using your developed course to answer this

with your prevailing cautions and precautions to regulate

such people positively and negatively.

The answer goes:

the necessary safety in going closer to your open and secret enemies are:

by going closer,

the possible reasons behind going against you will definitely

be identified and amendment should be made to that to avoid

such subsequently as some enemies are not merciful while

you never know how other of such category might be in future,

humans go for power only when their enemies are identified forgotten

that power is necessarily to be gained before any other thing,

only when you have enemies you are sure of your greatness

and it is widely known that going closer to your enemies will give you room

to know their secrets which aid their quick destructions in your hand

and getting closer to them will enable  to know your real and

unreal enemies in order not to waste time chasing wind.

On the other hand,

getting closer to them might give them room to quickly finish up

with you only if you are not adequately prepared,

the wiser ones might deceives you and

you might lose focus of discharging your earthly purpose

that give rise to evil heart against you.

Therefore, the best thing is to try as possible to

discharge your earthly purpose using maturity and understanding

to keep their full attention from you.

Because, it is when you are doing things with pride that others

might like fun to distract you.

Enemies are inevitable in life during discharging great desires.

They likewise strengthen human's efforts and also give courage

to humans to complete the work.

It is better to identify your enemies for that will give easy way

to go for knowledge that can help overcome them

in order to hasten your purpose manifestation.

If you are knowledgeable enough,

you can make them your friend attain defeating them or otherwise.

Because, not knowing your enemies might be more dangerous

as they might be in your opposite door.

Therefore, the course has pointed out the principles, laws, components

and the rest alike to identify the nature of human activities and

to see how possible ways to tackle and to get  dominant in any particular matter.

Second question,

how can someone make complete and partial negative effects from

good developed work and make the opposite relations with adequate final result

and how is it necessary to regain the former ground,

using the same effects?

Answer: everything in life has two parts.

The very thing that can create can also destroy.

The major thing needed is change of methods.

Out of good things we have bad things,

so as it is to the side.

One can simply recount his or her doings to get desire result at hand.

Effects are what matters,

effects go by calculations and as soon as the calculations are changed,

the content or the initial contents are equally changed.

Therefore, plans and methods changes contents.

So, if there are applied appropriately it yield good results whereas,

when there are applied inappropriately, it yield bad results.

Changes are constants.

So, it remain changing  towards your desire position

as long as you continue to change the components

and it is equally possible to regain the initial content as soon as

the earlier calculation resurface on the particular activities.

Even if you do not experience exact changes,

it should be definitely be similar, as usually.

Third question:

compare and constract the appropriation of different characters in relation to

different situations with safety and dangerous forensic analysis to that.

Answer: human is desirous in nature.

Desirous beings embrace any effective and effectual plans and methods

to gain such activities. Controversies come as soon as results

are not meeting up with the desire.

Changes are therefore liable to happen.

In this regards, dedicated and borrowed characters become the order of the day,

because, there are some inbuilt characters

that are not responsible enough to attract the desires.

However, it should be noted that whatsoever

is not yours can't be fully mastered and that might stand firm

to being out-of-hand problem in future and that can lead to destruction of former glory

It is therefore better to be mastery in a particular character before proudly using it.

All ways to get desire result is good, but as we do so,

we should equally dedicate time to master such characters

to give prevailing justification when matter arrives.

Question four:

what is good and bad in relation to your course;

identify their properties, components, effects to the humanity

on the various possible grounds.

Answer: everything is good and innocent at it initial position and stage.

Human transactions on it to make the desires vandalize a particular thing.

The some humans when the transaction do not yield expected results becomes bad

whereas they have expected results it becomes good.

This need to happen in order to create room for deeper and better learning.

Remember, everything is good and so as it is bad.

The effects are on the bases of personal calculations concerning it existence.

It is noted that the components of good things are:

right calculations and positive effects whereas

bad components are wrong calculations and negative effects.

Good things create room for enabling environment,

it manifests the glory of artworks and command growths and developments in humanity

whereas the bad things creates harmful environment,

destroys the glory of past and degrade humanity in plenty ways.

Their various properties are:

plans, methods, effects and influence.

Question five:

what is the relationship between time, death and life:

extend the results towards the growth and development of the humanity

and identify their various safety and dangers.

Answer:  the three are very powerful in humanity.

Because, without them, there will be no single growth and development.

Life is the determinant of the both.

Time is the dependent of death and death is the reason behind accurate

and adequate time which will be used by life.

In this regards, their glory and functions cover one another.

If there is no death,

life will not be serious at doing good things

and will not be in a haste to achieve some things.

If there is no time, life will not have time to do things.

And if there is no life, time and death are useless.

Therefore, the world would have not experience

any change or growth and development of any type without

the three phenomena of greatest positions.

On the other hand, their various safety and dangers depends

on one another as well due to their similar artworks.

Question six:

give beautiful examples and facts on how someone can draft powers,

maintain powers and distribute powers

to the necessary people in need using your course.

Answer: human being is very knowledgeable that is why

it is only human that have share in powers.

Power is acquired in a major percentage.

Humans can acquire power using money,

gathering people under him or her,

go to places that are necessary and doing things that are necessary.

It is a nature of human to retain or maintain power after it is given.

No one loves decrease rather increases of all size and types.

Therefore, as soon as human gains power,

he continues worshiping the source of his power so as to remain active with him.

It is also a nature of human to distribute

his or her acquired powers to whosoever he or she loves to simply aids representation

when and where needed.

This is done by taking the person along to where it is gained

or given the person the secrets to gain and uphold such particular power.

With me, the above questions which were answered

are the major and useful questions and answers from your ten submitted questions.

As you go deeper and better on this study,

I am very sure that,

you get to know more relevance of the course in humanity.

I will always be at door on coming for consultation.

As you come, there are some things that are there

to know more concerning your area of problem.

www.ingramcontent.com/pod-product-compliance
Lightning Source LLC
Chambersburg PA
CBHW030424160726
47992CB00007B/3275